OUR LADY
OF THE FLOWERS,
ECHOIC

CHRIS TYSH

with a preface by
Robert Glück

TRENCHART: LOGISTICS

♪

LES FIGUES PRESS

Los Angeles

Our Lady of the Flowers, Echoic
FIRST EDITION

Text design by Andrew Wessels and Teresa Carmody

ISBN 13: 978-1-934254-47-9
ISBN 10: 1-934254-47-9
Library of Congress Control Number: 2013938085

Les Figues Press thanks its subscribers for their support and reader-
ship. Les Figues Press is a 501c3 organization. Donations are
tax-deductible.

Les Figues would like to acknowledge the following individuals for
their generosity: Peter Binkow and Johanna Blakley, Lauren Bon,
Chris and Diane Calkins, Coco Owen, Dr. Robert Wessels, and
the Skyscrape Foundation.

Les Figues Press titles are available through:
Les Figues Press, <http://www.lesfigues.com>
Small Press Distribution, <http://www.spdbooks.org>

Special thanks to Katie Browne, Scott Lerner, Chelsea McNay,
Shoshana Seidman, and Emerson Whitney.

TrenchArt 8/1

Book 2 of 5 in the TRENCHART Logistics Series.

This project is supported in part by
a generous grant from the
National Endowment for the Arts.

ART WORKS.
arts.gov

Post Office Box 7736
Los Angeles, CA 90007
info@lesfigues.com
www.lesfigues.com

$(p+r)^n$

for Aaron Shurin
"the terrible pleasure of verse"

PREFACE FOR OUR LADY

Reading Chris Tysh's poem, *Our Lady of the Flowers, Echoic*, I am reminded of the days — my own days — when homosexuality was a sickness and a crime, and my flesh was dense with disease and guilt. Tysh's poem inevitably tests the difference between those days and these days. In fact, of the many translations that occur in this work, I wonder if translating the present into the past isn't foremost?

Next comes translating a novel into a poem, or more specifically, into stanzas. In the first place: a novel. In the first place: written inside a prison on brown paper used to make bags for occupational therapy. In the first place: an aid to masturbation, "For the enchantment of my cell" — the goal of many novels but few if any poems. Georges Bataille, ever the pedagogue, complained of the non-communicativeness of Genet's characters, but what exactly does one ask of an aid to masturbation? Sade, Genet, powerful masturbators, dead stars of the self who swallow the beams they emit. Those beams are a monstrance, glorying in divinity's presence. "Thus I live with the mystery / Of infinite holes in the shape of men."

Perhaps the only fully realized character in Genet's *Our Lady* is his "voice," and the isolation of that voice is the most profound experience of reading Genet. Tysh's poem translates that isolation. Tysh's self is more porous; it conveys affinity and a confusing intimacy. She confuses the personal pronoun and it's impossible (in a good way) to know how to take this couplet. "I could without changing much / Speak of my life right here and now." Let's say she proposes a self that comes to equal an uncertain reading. But like Genet, Tysh is something of a snake charmer, or the snake itself? — lyricism unfolding kaleidoscopically, extending emotions and meanings, fastening this mouse/reader to the spot.

Duality's pluses and minuses make a battery that powers Genet's novels. He turns hidden and visible on their heads, pure and impure, dirty and proper, loyalty and betrayal, *and so on*. What concerns Tysh most, I think, are the endlessly shifting relations of the original that seem to lift out of the text (maybe this is what Bataille meant by non-communication). The poem further detaches these relations from narrative consequence, suppressing the difference between figure and ground, and revealing instead overall patterns of gesture. Gestures become patterns that, taken together, are the continuous exchange that manufactures structures of gender and sexuality.

Tysh's poem adds a chapter to the practice of appropriation in that it conflates reading and writing, the way a cover (to a song) conflates listening to the original and making one's version. Tysh does not answer the plot but plays it again on her own instrument, which is her poetry, or more particularly her stanza. The writer/audience dynamics organized around the performance of self that characterize appropriation are replaced by a sense of vertigo before the act of creation. In that sense, I would call this project conceptual.

The great queen's mighty transformation into a woman must fail a little to allow the art to be witnessed. Homosexuals perfected the art of controlling our own invisibility. I long for the days when such stage effects really did make a performance. I would say that Tysh enlarges this proposition: artifice extends to the self, which controls its invisibility. The great queen exerts her revenge on time and space. Artifice leads to the truth of the self, and the truth is murder and guilt. "The astounding story where / A fake murder leads to a real / One."

Robert Glück
San Francisco, CA
2013

OUR LADY
OF THE FLOWERS,
ECHOIC[1]

[1] Source text: Jean Genet. *Notre-Dame-des-Fleurs*. Lyon: L'Arbalète, 1948; Paris, Gallimard, 1976. (Folio 860)

To be decapitated is to appear — banded, erect: like the "head swathed" (Weidmann, the nun, the aviator, the mummy, the nursling) and like the phallus, the erectile stem — the style — of a flower.

Jacques Derrida

On the news Weidmann, his head
Like a nun in white or a wounded
Pilot, falls down in silky rye
The same day Our Lady of the Flowers
Stamped all over France dangles his crimes
By a golden string — nimble assassins mount
The back stairs of our sleep

There were others, of course, orphaned
Fragments I overhear prisoners sing
Inside when voices rise in psalm
From the depths of their misery
Each time my heart bangs like it did
When the German dropped his bomb
And I smiled, a tiny sign between us

It can't be pure chance that I cut out
Those handsome heads with empty
Eyes or rather sky-blue windows
On the construction site not yet up
Who said vacant? When their eyes do close
It's creepier than a viper's nest to the girl
Who walks by the barred spy-hole

That each cell becomes where strange types
Crash, swear and dream on straw pallets
Or maybe something of a confession
Booth with its dark screen. Empty
Theatres, deserted prisons, idle machinery
Those eyes hold me entranced and I feel
My way, groping along like a blind man

Until in wild panic I arrive by a sordid alley
Face to face with nothing but a void
Propped and swollen like a huge foxglove
The papers torn, sheared of their pimps
Like a May garden looted of its blossoms
It is you I remember at night: stretched
Like a coffin at sea, pale and wintry

You flow into me, white blessed body
Now a halo, supernatural cocoon
You prick with both your feet.
Out of chewed bread I make glue
For my cutouts — some I pin with brass wire
That inmates use for funereal wreaths
Now star-shaped frames for the criminal

Element. I live here among ruins
Smiles or pouts all enter through
My open pores, myself, my family.
To give them their due, their retinue
I've added a few profiles from those
Cheap paperbacks we smuggle in the yard:
Young half-breed or Apache with a hard-on

Under the sheets I choose my nightly
Outlaw, caress his absent face
Then the body which resists at first
Opens up like a mirror armoire
That falls out of the wall and pins me
On the stained mat where I think
Of God and his angels come at last

With the help of my unknown lovers —
Nobody can say when and if I'll get out —
I'll compose a story: my heroes are
Stuck on the wall and I in lockdown
As you read about Divine and Culafroy
You might at times hear lines mixed in
With a drop of blood, an exclamation point

In the drowsy morning as the screw
Throws in his low "Bonjour"
The fact of a few pink girls, now white
Corpses, flows through
An ineffable fairytale I tell
In my own words
For the enchantment of my cell

Divine died yesterday
In a pool of blood more red
You would see Jesus' oriflamme
Flying for The Sacred Heart
Her lungs like a piece of evidence
In the judge's chamber squeezed shut
Now it rains behind bars, wind too

A spiral stairway leads to the attic
Overlooking a small Montmartre
Cemetery where D lived for a spell
It will be the anteroom of her crypt
Thick with putrid flowers and incense
Floor to floor it rises toward death
And then at the top no more

Than a phantom shadow
Tinged with blue while outside
Let's say under the black canopy
Of tiny umbrellas, Mimosa I,
Mimosa II, Mimosa half-IV,
First Communion, Angela, Her
Highness, Castagnette and Régine

Await holding sprays of violets
All the queens, boys and girls
Are there knotted together chattering
And tweeting, pearl tiaras on their heads
I let myself sink to my old village grave-
Yard where snails and slugs leave
Trails of slime on white flagstones

"Poor darling!" "Can you beat it?"
"She was losing it." "Where's Mignon?"
Any minute now there'll be a black horse
Procession and the rest by way of Rachel
Avenue. Oh the scene! The Eternal makes
His entrance, smiling, supple and elegant
Without a hat. They call him Mignon-Dainty-Feet.

In the rectangle of my door I thought
I saw him once like a dead man walking
On pricey furs. In a flash, I'm his
Discharged to the core — not a dab of self
Remains but ruffian, pimp and gangster
He's lodged instead, his lacy fingers —
Baby Jesus in its crib — receive the world

As he moves through the queens
Like a shiny slaughterhouse knife
They part and recast in silence
Their traveling line — two at a time
He runs up the steps, lifted, I'd have
Said, to the house of death now real
As tears, flowers and mourning veil

Old Ernestine, Divine's mother
Though still a beauty was done for
Having ransacked a thousand and one
Roles from pulp novels that corrupt
The real: gun in gloved hand
She stages her son's dénouement
The way others shoot up smack

With a crystal spike
The room slides like a diamond
On her index finger into gold
Velvet and walnut-paneled walls
"I feel it, Lou's hour has come,"
She moans using the boy's old name
Buried axe at the bottom of a pool

The whole construction bound
To shatter her nerves, feeling faint
Amid hangings, beveled mirrors
And gloom's infernal ruckus
In two seconds flat, she recovers her cool
Would go first lighter than thought
And wait by the coffin, gray shape now

That's how Mignon saw her
Drunk with grief like a Queen
Of Spades, black widow of dry
Wings spread across the bed
Curtains, walls and rugs that wear
Death's private seal stamped low
On the parchment. Some stray dogs

Like to repeat such news, scent of sulfur
In the air — already Mignon forgets the pad
He shared with D, will not linger near the lacy
Shroud. He's simply drifting about.
Outside, a black cortège, rouge and blush
Finally arrives by the pit already dug
And Divine is no more: dead and buried

Among cries and girly giggles.
Divinaria, D's saga, will be the tale
I trace in the starless subterranean sky
Switching genders as if passing under
A nightclub's scarlet awning where I steal
A glance at some elfin gypsy with hair
Covered in dew and river marsh

Limpid water to the shapeless mud of others
Divine enters Graff's café at two a.m.
Fresh scent of scandal at her heels
Heads turn: bankers, gigolos and scarecrows
Her public life starts now: alone at a table
A ceremony with black tea and a pair
Of pants stolen from a sailor.

Her seduction will be implacable
Finer than amber and yet she's kin
To the prowlers at fairgrounds
Who with a flick of their wrists
Set slot machines and trail behind them
The fatal lacework of magic city
She crosses her legs and smiles

She's cruising tonight and no dice
If it were up to me I'd give her marble
Hips, polished cheeks and pagan knees
From which to climb toward Pigalle
Picture her on a bench, a hint of leg
And a column of smoke rising
"They're crazy about me, those nights

Oh the sultanas! My God, they're
Tickling my ass, the cheeky girls."
Some mornings, men wake up gasping
So horny they'd swallow their own hand
To be done with wanting. Divine is hungry
In the empty streets only a few rowdy teens
Insert a stripe of sound, undone shoelaces

Dragging behind. It's understood
She won't score tonight. Just then
A man bumps into her. "I'm so sorry."
"No problem," says the queen. It is
Mignon-Dainty-Feet: 5'9", 165 lbs, blond,
Blue-green eyes, perfect teeth, oval face,
10-inch prick, and as young as D

When I knew her in the joint at Fresnes
She'd talk about him, deep swell prone
To exaggerate the sumptuous contours
Of his face I never met in person and now
Must borrow a thing or two from a thug
I call Roger in my head as we're bound
Together by the make-believe ring of crime

I'm worn out and my wrist has a cramp
Like a Tour de France cyclist I give up
The race and yet certain details foretell
I shall wear his crown but now surrender
To Mignon, a little drunk, as he plows
Into D in that chancy dawn that starts
Our tale, inside out, phantom frame

Having ascended high above the sea
Like a crow's nest from where D shakes
Her dust rag and bids adieu to ghosts
They find themselves tangled up
In the damp sails of an avalanche
"Boy, I was really wasted last night,"
He laughs taking in the scene

From the way he speaks, lights
His cigarette, D knows him for a pimp
Like a bird they say that flies
Into a serpent's mouth, she goes
"Stay, I mean, if you want to."
Among the stolen radio wires, shabby
Rugs and lamps, a life begins

As is the habit, Divine will hustle
On Place Blanche while Mignon
Takes in a show. Under his advice
She thrives, knowing whom to roll
And whom to blackmail in the daily
Protocol where coke lends a hazy hand
Bodies float, untouchable

I must insist on Mignon's looks
Undoubtedly a thug he carries
Bits of light that trail like ivy on a stele
A pedestal half-hidden with flowers
He's been pissing on since boyhood:
Legs spread, knees slightly bent
"I've dropped a pearl," he says

Black eyes for most mac daddies
A matter of shame — for Mignon:
"My two violet posies" or when
The need seizes him: "I've got
A cigar at the tip of my lips."
D knows nothing yet about this
Business of ratting out her friends

To the cops. For now he keeps
His traitor mug to himself
It's not that he approves but
The caress is so much sweeter
Who's about to pull a job
The inspector asks — 100 francs
In your piggybank, snap!

Stool pigeon that's me! Mignon walks
Down Rue Dancourt high on his own
Abjection lest its intensity kill him
Felt hat, plaid suit, shoulders back
His tie a flame and those outrageous
Yellow pointy shoes peculiar to macs
He steals their thunder, all smiles

After two stints in jail he imagines
The effect each new outfit will have
On the boys. Prison is a savage god
To whom he offers gold watches, pens,
Rings and scarves. He dreams less
Of strutting his stuff with ladies than
Entering a cell in a white silk shirt

Open at the neck. That is the shape
Of the fate he bows to, maybe since
He once read, scrawled in a john
A tag about *Martin the Faggot*,
Bob the Queer and *Li'l Meadow*
The Swish. It's hard not to wish
His name were up there, cursive temple

Of felons. Accursed would do more
Justice, I think — there comes a day when
One tires of the hero stance and snitches
To be back in the sandbox with other cast-
Offs, but for now Divine drinks her tea
Like a dove while Mignon, hands in pockets,
Does his cha-cha: three steps, shuffle and back

Each stolen object: liquor, perfume,
Fake jewelry, gives the room its
Mysterious allure like flashing
Lights on a distant ship. Parked car
Or friend's pocket, Mignon will boost
Anything anywhere and D will simply
Say, I feel like praying on his bare chest

On Sundays they go to mass, gold
Clasp missal in D's hand, clickety-
Clack they kneel on plush pews
And let a mean-looking priest
Cram the host into their mouths
"Our Mother Who Art in Heaven,"
They pour out in unison, bow down

To the splendor of the pious world
At home, Mignon dives into D
As into a mirror — a silent key opens
The door and he becomes the sea
Monster then solid rock where
Andromeda, chained naked, must
Lie under a ravaged sky, mindful

Of the man who lets her drink
A sip of tea, lips pressed together
Pass it back to him, etc. …
At the Roxy bar he likes to play
Poker dice, his gestures strike
A timeless pose rolling a cigarette
Uncapping a fountain pen

How sweet it is to speak
Of those two at the precise
Moment when planes are
Sobbing and the whole world
Is running amok before gun-
Fire. Already the soldiers'
Flesh droops like a half moon

While I dream of the lovers' garret
And the ways love surprises
People's lives like a walk-on part:
Two young wrestlers huddle together
Tangled hair, open shirts, they rewrite
The score high up in the Milky Way
Other constellations take shape:

Boxer, Violin, Dagger and Sailor
A whole new map of heavens outlined
On D's wall where she throws her cum
At the sight of a cherry blossom strangely
Black and stiff in its vase, D the farm girl
That she is, feels the cut like a murdered child
Mignon couldn't care less, gives a horselaugh

In return. Blows follow, land and slide
Softly. There's something off-putting to D
About fighting back, that grimace
Of a raised fist and knitted brows
Leaves her cold — too butch in a word
Like whistling with two fingers in your mouth
Or pulling up one's pants, both hands at once

Slang belonged to men, the queens liked
To think, intrinsic rights of a warrior
His crest and spurs. Fairies have their own
Idiom. One day standing at the bar, Mimosa
Dares, "His screwy tale…"
And pisses everybody off
"Broad acting tough," someone spits

Bit of tobacco caught between his lips
The argot that curls their tongues
Makes D weak in the knees, little gasps
Like a hand on a fly
Their pig latin — eddbay, allbay— and derailed speech
"Go, you're cured," the pimps would say
Meaning all's well that ends well. Beat it!

At dawn, Divine hears church bells
And returns in her mind to a small
Rainy town three or four years ago
When, still Culafroy, he roamed the streets
And slept on a bench with other derelicts
All fraternal souls in the eternal dreary morning
Squeezed by destiny

The child that preoccupies us is invisible
Train stations or docks, cops see squat
Even in jail, he seems to have been smuggled in
Like smokes, razor blades or the air of a phonograph
Spellbound, the runaway kid can't sleep a lick
Walks around shadowy streets peering at cupids
And altars — such a gilded world in its magic wig

Next to Mignon's furnace body, D grows
Cold, remembering the young vagabond stumble
Against bums and debris while she sleeps
In the husk of their married selves
This morning, the ghost of my dream or rather
Its corpse, now no bigger than a king's epiphany
Cake, floats in the air, serene like a baptism

I go back to bed and wait for chow.
To enter the precise and tangible world
Of my cell is out of the question now
Mignon, Divine, I'm all alone here
True or not, you will have guessed
That in the end it's my own destiny's coat
I drape on D's shoulders — tatters or courtly mantle

As I dart around, turning D into a saint
The reader will have to improvise his own
Notion of time and duration. Beyond good
And evil, I take her by the hand and lead,
Poor angel that I am, toward luxury
D learns from the inside by touching
Like a blind man: marble, rugs, ebony

When her hired car passes by a wrought-
Iron gate or traces a silent figure-eight
On the gravel, Divine is most an infanta
Up her sleeve, she carries a small fan
Made of muslin and ivory that she unfurls
Over her chin, flashing between two words
"He's dumb as a doorknob," Mimosa adds

A little tipsy, Divine's taken to the station
In front of a crowd scattered on the Boulevard
"Lock'er up and throw away the key," they chant
Next day she's back to her spot, one eyelid
Blue and swollen. "Sweet Jesus, girls,
I about died the way those cops wiped my face
Like Holy Women."

Each bust is always the first I realize
As soon as my hands are caught
In their steel coupé
More dazzling than a theorem
The raw consolation 24/7
Of piss, formaldehyde and sweat
Beneath the coarse wool blankets

Divine and Mignon, to my mind
The ideal lovers. He a giant
Whose feet cover half the globe
His boner so huge and calm
Sexes slip like rings on a finger
You'd think young warriors, June 14th
1940, buggering us all as they march

In the dusty sun. I close my eyes.
For Mignon, D is barely a pretext
But for Divine he's everything:
Her joystick, little pony, love missile
Jesus in his manger, baby brother
An object of pure luxury that she decks
Out with ribbons and flowers

When Mimo pays a visit, she and D
Kiss on the cheek. "I just love your
Pad," she says, "it's like a priest's home
All that green in the back. Must be
Sweet to sleep with those ghosts nearby."
The cemetery was like a liquid eye
In a black man's palm

It had entered D's soul the way certain
Phrases enter a text, a letter here, a letter there
At the window, Mimosa, looking for a grave
Yells out, "Bitch, you finally croaked, six
Feet under while I walk on your head, whore!"
Mignon, who's about to ditch D, looks around
A strange crumbly smile on his lips

Mimosa's man, Roger, had joined the army
She's gone to war, she had told Mignon
Who offered, for kicks, to replace him
And that was that. Our households, our
Loves don't look like yours. Without
Batting an eyelash nor a drop of remorse
He'd decided to split from D

Without wanting to spoil the effect
Let us come close to the scene
Where the treacherous queen
Tweets on as if she hadn't just
Plunged her dagger into D's heart
"When it's still inside and bulges
Along the crease that goes on and on

You'd think the Belle strolled off
A cruise ship, no kidding," she croons
Cutting her eyes at Mignon
Who steps into the puddle
Of their giddy fag speech
Like a jewelry thief, shadowy
"No news from your Roger man?"

"I'm the Quite-Alone," she whispers
Her ring finger holding at bay
An invisible storm: eyes, teeth,
Mouth, everything that has to do
With the exuberance of voice and gesture
Veiled and gloved in a mysterious sheen
Divine knows the score though she'll forget

At times to hold her tongue in front
Of the macs, Place Clichy, and Mignon
Will have to school her with two slaps
Ouch! She's no taller than the zinc bar
Scram! He's fuming under the green neon
The queens telegraph each other, "I'm the
Q-Q," meaning the Quite-Quite

Looking for a reason to quarrel
With Divine, Mignon finds none
Calls her a slut and leaves the attic
Now that she's alone, what will I do?
Shall I give her that gypsy kid, fresh
Off the boat, with his tall pumps and sailor
Pants that cup his butt like a public bench?

Let it be known we love without
Sacrament nor morals
Our laws are stitched in the raw
Malfeasance of the one who blows
A hole in his bridal bed after six moons
For fun, trailing behind him the immense
Aura of scorn for all square things, bonds, etc.

What I need now is to pull out the rug
From under D, watch as she falls and breaks
Her neck from the mezzanine floor, or put
Another way, blow up her image
Then cut and press together into the sheets
Of my notebook when I'm good and ready
So that only a hint of her essence remains

Hence D's fan found in the hallway
By Mr. Roquelaure as he returns
With *Le Petit Parisien* and a bottle
Of milk. That very night Divine
Runs into Mignon quite by chance
Not a word about who ditched whom
Nor why. He whistles, a tad contrite

Mimosa flies up from nowhere
Her wild voice suddenly male
To D's ears: "Get the fuck out
You dirty whore, cocksucker!"
Mignon, splendid once more
In his cowardice which frames him
Like a white halo, stands aside

"Go ahead, kill each other,"
He says, "See if I care."
I still hear his mean laughter
Like a street fanfare
A showy rain of kicks and blows
Descends from top to bottom
Though most of D's end in the air

When all is said and done, life
Returns to normal in the ballad
Of Montmartre above the dead
Pity me! I'm pushing thirty
My head swaddled in romance
While I rot in the joint, God picks
Daisies for his mystic throne

In the game of self-contempt
I've become a master, gold
Medal hanging from a ribbon
Were I to say I'm nothing
But an old whore, who's to up
The ante on the table of tar and feather
Below which I lie lowest of all

Divine and I play by the same
Rules that make us don the fluffy
Boas and gaudy tinsel of a feeling
Separate from its truth. We simply
Swallow the injury and smile with
Our accordion mouths no matter what
Mignon-the-adorable-cheat does

That's the only way I can love him
Borne out of stone indifference
The very same sentence D will apply
To Our Lady of the Flowers
Who makes his formal entrance
Here, dear reader, through the back-
Door of crime where he waits

Like a bridegroom in white gloves
"Who's there?" the old man asks
"It's me," our 16-year-old replies
Strange how easy it is to kill
As the heart lines up straight in front
Of the weapon and the neck finds a resting
Place between the assassin's joined hands

The old man lies dead on a blue rug
I listen to the chimes that flood his head
You'd think the teen was running
From grove to grove on an April road
Orange blossom in his velvet buttonhole
Where the fuck does he stash his dough?
Our Lady pounds and scrapes in vain

In the midst of objects that have lost
All meaning, a monstrous sieve
Through which pass the dead souls
Of furniture. He panics. Get the hell
Out! The cops will be here any minute!
Just then he bumps into a vase: twenty
Thousand francs flutter to his feet

Air. Crystal. Nocturnal silence
He walks for all eternity, toward
A small hotel for tricks and johns
In the rented room he comes face
To face with that first rise of nausea
Many convicts have told me about
The dead man flows in your veins

Seeps out of your eyes, ears and mouth
Wild flowers bursting through a corpse
To shake off the stiff, really to vomit him
Our Lady holds himself, first light as a bird
Then his assassin's hand circles the crown
Hard. The night disappears at the rim of sleep
Let the young murderer be my haunted castle

Pilorge is the one I think of most
Sprawled out on the cover of *Détective
Magazine*. Face, somber like a forest
On a stormy night, you will need no ladder
To ascend the guillotine. The others are already
There: Weidmann, Sun Angel, Soclay.
I've dreamed my share of deaths

Our Lady of the Flowers comes
From the same wall stippled
With sun and shadow as fear
Stretches his limbs, gives his smile
A bluish tint and the sensation of floating
Impossibly svelte in that spectral gray
Flannel suit of his

He wore the day of the crime
And that he'll wear the day he dies
Right now he's at Gare St. Lazare
Buying a ticket for Le Havre
It takes him no more than a second
To realize that he's dropped his fat
Wallet and Mignon's picked it up

The sound of each bill as he counts
Under his breath and pockets ten
Squinting like a Chicago gangster —
That's his template or maybe a crook
From Marseille — and then unbelievably
Returns the rest to Our Lady of the Flowers
I'll let you imagine their dialogue

Go ahead. Be my guest. Think the wildest
Schemes hanging on a thread of slang
They exchange in a brotherly embrace
Mignon orders a suit for both of them
Shoes and the whole nine yards that give
A man that special charm. Two small hoods
In search of gold cruising Avenue Wagram

And then one day, inevitably, Our Lady
Confesses his crime. Mignon returns
The favor with Divine, although he can't
Quite choke the old gag of ratting out his pals
Mixed in the silent drama of abetting
And a tender feeling for this teenage thief
Still, the kid better explain his wacky name

Little by little he comes to it
With such strain that the marble
Serpents coiled in his face
Awake and the name enters the room
"You see, the guys used to call me that …"
Mignon understands that the smallest
Sign, even discernible breath, will destroy him

Bowled over by his effort, the young
Assassin sinks into the vile mud
I'd like to transform into a bed of roses
Or, better yet, an altar bathed in light
Help! Mignon, Divine, Our Lady,
Stay! I cry waving both of my arms
But a terrible dream sweeps all cells

Like a giant crocodile made up
Of guards' mouths and judges' chests
And the poisoned air of jail
Swallows me whole very slowly
I appear before the judge, white
As a sheet on which I sign my confession
Sure that I'll be pardoned

What have I done? my lawyer asks
In shock. Was I nuts? No way
To take it back, undo the ball of twine
That traced the path from my icy cell
To the black corridors of the courthouse
Maybe I can seduce the guard who drags me
By the wrist? I'm as good as dead, my friends

At death's door, one foot in the grave
The sands of life are running out
At certain moments one truly grasps
What is meant by such expressions
The visceral vertigo that precedes
Falling from a precipice, everything
Goes black before the final shock

Not even a stony arm to catch me
And yet back in box 426 I drink in
The sweet fullness of my work
Its soothing comfort as if the mind
Deep inside was a footprint
I walk along inch by inch, transfixed,
Though I stumble more than once

Twenty thousand francs at the Palace
Won't last forever, Mignon must
Be thinking of returning to Divine
Now that their dough is gone
Dressed like two fake kings
Our Lady and Mignon collapse
Heads and shoulders at her feet

Divine, who until now has only
Loved macho guys, feels like a
New blade of grass is pushing up
From the earth. She falls hard
For Our Lady's flower face and
Begins the slow apprenticeship
Of masculinity

She whistles, hands in pockets
Imagines her arms and legs
On the body of a boxer
Striking a pose she builds
Like a puzzle, dashing from
Girl to boy. In the end, space cadet,
she forgets her lessons

To seal in the new switch
She dreams up a friendship
With a real pimp where each
Gesture is plain as a rock
Stiff bearer of truth
She'll name Marchetti
Assembled for the occasion

From an endless catalogue
Of thighs, torsos, knees and hair
She keeps ready for her lonely nights
If you read below the line you'll see
Each of these constructs hatched
By her desire — her hunger
Up close shows the same soul:

The very one she would've liked
To have. Once invented, Marchetti
Plays his part to a T, until one night
She pretends to be tired of Our Lady
And please can you take him off
My hands. They shake on it.
"No sweat!" One man to another

But instead of more virile
Divine just turns old, dry bones
Like an ivory crucifix beginning
To lose its sheen, she'll scream
If you turn on the light
The least shadow sends her trembling
Sirens' invitation to death

It's the season of tears
The way we speak of
The season of rains
The joy that signals
Suicide. Before you
Know it, she's blushed
For a yes or no

The-Very-Crimson turned on
By an adolescent! It's not the job
That shames her, after all, she's
Been drinking from that cup a thousand
Years, Miss Whore to you, good folks,
It's the little scraps others find harmless
That slice her veins and let the words

Fly from their coffins. Even as Culafroy
She dreads their power to bring her down
To the lowest rung. Let us steal a glance
At that era of Divine's life which holds
The immense Sahara of his childhood
Under a widening sun steeped in poison.
In short pants and schoolboy smock

He cries, sad little sovereign,
The makeshift violin that Ernestine
Refused to buy, all gone now
Nothing but broken white chords
And a broomstick handle, he's kicked
The whole lot under the floor from where
Thin specters of sound come to haunt his sleep

Everything about the village is strange
Like an invitation to watch a cortège
Of First-Communion girls with porcelain
Heads crowned in flowers and choirboys
Swinging censers under a noonday sun
Toward evening, one might see their elder
Sisters carry stillborns in narrow pine

Varnished like violin cases
Then at a crawl up a tree, boys
Would press their naked bellies
To feel the sap, all skin, earth, sky.
Rye, pine, clover stand upside down
In the moonlight lake. Divine's child-
Hood — at least some of it — looks like that

Let's say she's never feared God, Jesus
Nor the Holy Virgin, not like their wrath,
Contempt for her brand of loving
Until Gabriel makes the scene. I see him
Walking down a street, almost running
Bumping into D as the doorbell rings twice
Above the little candy store he's ducked into

I want to talk about those chance meetings
I provoke within the book like a surprise
Dollar package one buys for tots: that
Single instant when I glance at the busy
Street, a strange tenderness in my heart
I'm charmed. My gaze returns and all's
Gone. Thus, Divine meets Gabriel.

Like a cliff or glass wall his back
Arches, black wings of an eagle
Fly out above the shadows.
Gabriel is a foot soldier dressed
In sky-blue. We'll sketch him
Later when he stands off to the side
Of our story. Naturally, D will call him

Archangel. For fear of Mignon
She sees him in town and at once
Knows that he's a branch of her life
An underground vein. "You're not
My friend. You are my heart, myself,"
She says to him. He smiles, "Damn!"
Tickled pink by such worship.

All the way from Blanche
To Pigalle they walk as if blessed
In matrimony by the rabble
That twitters on their passage
Sick with fear the old queen
Dreams of war maneuvers
A parade in the forbidden city

It had to happen! One day she invites
Gabriel upstairs to rehearse a role
Equal in length to her longing: blinds drawn
She pretends she's just awoken. "Sit down."
His coarse wool uniform is a measure,
Even proof that she remembers the black cloth
Of country priests and state orphans.

"Doesn't that itch?" she asks. Later she'll say,
"Those pants, what a turn-on!"
"You're nuts! I got drawers on; the wool doesn't
Even touch my skin." Divine, I've said it
Before, is clad in blue which bends around
Her pale body like a tongue thrown in lament:
"I'm getting old, pushing thirty."

Gabriel has the courtesy not to flatter
Her with a lie: "That's the true age."
Two angels on a wire tired of flying
Now tossed by wind into a field
Of nettles couldn't be more chaste
But comes a night when the Archangel
Turns faun: he rips her open, half

Man half horse, their teeth part
Gleaming in the night, skin and eyes
Now lighter than ash or salt
D swoons with love like a nymph in a tree
Then whoosh! he's gone and dead at war
Buried where he fell by the Chateau
Of Touraine. She can visit his grave

In the narrow circle of her solitude
D wouldn't leave the attic for days
And nights on end; blinds drawn
On the Bay of the Dead, she lies
In bed drinking tea, feeling old —
Hollowed eyes, hair plastered
Under a wig — the queen can't help

To descend, in between fits of blue,
The strict periphery of her being
Until she finds what she's looking
For: in the childhood stream there
Stands Alberto with his heavy leather
Pouch, a puckering smile that D paints
With her own mouth

"You wanna touch'em," the Snake
Charmer says. "Go ahead, they won't
Hurt you," Alberto adds, showing
Three vipers writhing about, their dark
Heads a tangle of cowls, icy scales
Glistening in the petrified light
Like a spark, revelation falls on him

At the very moment Alberto's hand
Finds the hissing thing gliding under
His fingertips, suddenly more feeling
Than ever before like those tiny fleshy
Bumps the blind use to decipher Braille
It seems to Lou just then that he could
Swallow a whole mess of snakes as long

As Berto's hand doesn't leave his
Divine now shudders at the very thought
The long syllables of her boyhood name
Forever coiled in the maiden space that starts
Her knowing: an imperceptible trace, a cube
Of silence wild enough to blow up the church
God is hollow like Marie Antoinette's plaster

Bust that sat on the mantle in the blue slate house
Or the little lead soldiers my cellmate Clément
Paints, minuscule warriors hard as corpses
That sometimes tie me down with their Lilliputian
Sad stories and then to get loose I have to offer D
In exchange. Thus I live with the mystery
Of infinite holes in the shape of men.

I've got to come back to myself, my life
As a convict, the veins, the bones of it
When really I'd wished for nothing more
Than to show you a book laden with flowers
Snowy skirts and pale blue ribbons. The world
Of the living is too far away, ghostly shreds
The poor country boys don at carnival

I'm haunted by signs: circles, orbs,
Billiards, Venetian lanterns, soccer
Ball of the goalie in his orange jersey.
What's the worst that can happen other
Than what will happen? And yet I'm scared
As if I were a cadaver pursued by the cadaver
That I am. Jackal, fox, the whole animal

Reign holds court down below
I need a dream, a poem to shatter
The walls of my prison. Swallows
Nest in my armpits; if you look away
For a second, a young murderer appears
A silk hanky in his buttonhole, he's just
Come back from a night of dives with sailors

And whores, and doesn't know it's his crystal
Flesh my eyes probe as if all those points
Of light traced a pontoon, temporary bridge
To an elsewhere so real my naked feet slide
On the freshly washed deck (what deck? you
Must be mad, there's nothing but flat stones
And the tears I mistake for roses). The end.

Meanwhile outside, Divine finds herself
In one of those narrow bars hurried by
The promise of a tryst. At the other tables
The queens all chichi and nasty tongues
Crane their necks to better see D's coronet
Of fake pearls. Judith bows to the floor
"My respects, Madame!"

"Up yours!" Divine shoots back.
"Die Puppe hat gesprochen," someone says.
As she bursts out laughing, the crown falls
And breaks. In the general mirth that ensues
"The D is dethroned!" "Sunk," "Fallen from
High On," "Poor exile!" On the sawdust floor
The little pearls look just like those we thread

Through miles of brass wire to make
Funeral wreaths, which in turn resemble
Those that lay around my childhood
Cemetery, rusty and busted, what's left
After wind and rain but a pink porcelain
Angel with blue wings
In the bar the girls sink to their knees

Only the men stand. Then D raises
A strange strident laugh and sudden
As a card trick rips out her dental plate
Only to set it on her skull and with a
Changed voice, lips eating dust, says,
"Get this, ladies, I'm still a fucking queen."
It took incomparably more soul to replace

The bridge back in her mouth.
How shall we explain that D is now
Thirty, same age as me, of course
From twenty to twenty-seven
There came a period of deep luxury
When she led the sinuously complicated
Life of a kept woman

There were cruises on the Mediterranean
A gilded hotel in Vienna, Venice, Rome
A Renaissance château and more
All this I imagine in such intimate detail
The vexations of my cell surrender without
A word. From time to time, D comes back
To us, noble châtelaine, she sends Mignon

Money-orders, sometimes even jewelry
He wears at night before fencing it
To treat his pals to a spread
Finally back in Paris she preens and ruffles
Amidst our gestures, thinks she strews
Roses and peonies like the village girls used
To do on the day of Corpus Christi

How is it possible that the blackest world
The most charred and dismal, the severe
Naked night of factory workers, their bodies
Bent by machinery be entwined with marvel
That very thing we call popular song lost in the wind
Where we touch words of such ferocious wealth
Their vowels slash like a ruby dagger, the way

They sing with grave mouths or maybe
Whistle, hands in their pockets, insouciant
The parts about . . . marble steps . . . garden
Of roses . . . exquisite pink . . . deep inside
I tremble before the jagged thorns and
Beauty bush that adorn them as if
They bloomed on a theater poster

Speaking of singing, of popular
Literature so light because unwritten
Flying from mouth to mouth so hungry
For those expressions we dream of using:
"Little shit," "monkey-face," "pretty thug,"
In the twinkling of an eye we possess
The solid body of ten thousand hoods

Let it be said that runaway kids
All claim to have been mistreated
They know how to embroider this
Excuse with such singular detail
That everything we ever remember
From novels and news stories
About children kidnapped, tortured,

Sold, abandoned, raped and abused
Rushes at us and even the most suspicious
Folks like cops and judges will simply say
"One never knows."
For his fugue Lou invents a mean stepmother
They put him in jail out of habit
He's never seen anything so filthy

In a corner of his cell under a heap
Of dirty blankets, a kinky brown head
Laughs out loud: You AWOL from home?
Come on, you can talk here, we're among men
He shakes his brown rags which rattle like scrap
Iron. Help me with this leg, will you?
The little hoodlum had a wooden leg

Fastened to a stump with straps and buckles
Lou had the same aversion to infirmities as
He had for reptiles. The other kid frees up
A thigh and with a supreme effort
As if putting his hand on a flame
Lou touches the wood and finds himself
Clasping the apparatus close to his chest

The children sleep. As a species of
Punished outcasts, they are later
Transferred to a reformatory
Lou-Divine squats in his cell all day
And listens to the other little tramps
Whose vocabulary hugs shadowy
Alleys and scaled walls

Amidst this world of imps and fauns
The nuns float by like ballerinas
On poofy skirts and wag their heads
In silence
In spite of his tendency to daydream
He quickly becomes one of them
A vagabond picked up on the road

He doesn't want to disappoint
And lends a hand to a petty theft
When Mother Superior asks him why
"Because the others thought me a thief,"
Is all he can say in response
The night swells above the hammocks
A jungle full of pestilence, stone monsters

From above, the dorm looks unchanged
Everything happens below the covers
Which seem to wrap around sleepers
In little groups the kids crawl out
And light cigarettes thin as straw
Draw up plans for escape, all doomed to fail
A secret kingdom of peers and commoners

A thousand little jabs with a fine needle
Draw blood and trace the most
Extravagant figures, this nocturnal
Tattooing, sacred hieroglyphs on white skin
Sometimes eyelids, armpits, even the soles
Of feet are marked with crude signs
Moons, snakes, boats and pierced hearts

It's the nuns' habits that suggest
An escape plan to Culafroy
Hanging in the workroom as they do
With stockings and coifs for nights
On end, they whisper as if they've
Done nothing else but hatch narrow
Routes of cutting loose

Please save your loud outcry
What follows is quite improbable
But truth is not my strong suit
Towards midnight two kids
Help themselves to the clothes
And step into the dark street
In their own wooden shoes

The peasants hardly notice
Maybe just a touch of wonder
At seeing these two short nuns
Their grave faces hurry along
On the open road
The sovereignty of hunger
Leads the way quicker than fear

I'm not done talking about D
In her attic between Our Lady,
Guileless heart of marble, and Gorgui
Whom she leaves together while
Cruising for old johns
Had she been a woman only
Little would she care but Divine

Is *also* a man. Easy to imagine
An afternoon picture show
Where hands touch in the dark
Later they'll get a beer and head on
Home. Crack! go the caps
She's strewn along the sidewalk
Under Gorgui's steel toes, sparks fly

All three are about to step out
A cigarette on each mouth
With a kitchen match D
Sets fire to her own stake
Lights up Our Lady's and holds
The flame to Gorgui
"That's bad luck," he says

She lets the match fall, now weary
Face all dark and skinny as a dragonfly
"You start with a tiny superstition
And end up falling in God's arms."
Or a priest's bed, Our Lady thinks
Without saying the words
Top of Rue Lepic lies *The Tabernacle*

Little cabaret I've talked about before
His Eminence is in charge — the very one
Who used to say, "I make'm cry every night"
Meaning the safes he jimmied with a crowbar
You'll find them all there but mostly Banjo,
1st-Communion, Agnes, Mimosa and Divine
And their gents

Under the low ceiling handsome butcher
Boys sometimes pass in floor-length gowns
The men play poker dice.
A phonograph and we dance
Nothing but giddy drag queens
Rubbing against teen pimps
A dreamboat for murder, don't you think?

Divine has dug up two silk dresses:
A black sheath with sequins
She will wear herself and a pale
Blue faille with a bustle for Our Lady
"Are you nuts?"
In his eyes he sees his pals
Have a fit but none will snicker

Naked under the tight dress, he's captured
By the mirror, butt sticking out
Like two cellos
They're at the door
Spangled tulle fan and all
Let's just pin a velvet bud
On that tousled hair. There!

At the club it's a riot
Of muslin and flounces
Our Lady's buddies go wild
Between the downy skin
And the feel of silk
There's no telling how
He'll hide going hard

Under the stretched cloth
"Let me ditch this," he says
To Gorgui a little pink and wet
Around the eyes
Beyond them, the crowd rips
Like a sheer handkerchief
As Seck Gorgui — mighty

Thighs, shoulders rolling
Forward — clasps our killer close
Hands make a feathery nest
On his heart and off they go
On their flying carpet
Waltz, tango till dawn
Divine could cry with rage

A dragon or better yet a vampire
Strange how no one sees
Her front teeth lengthen nor the bony
Fingers scrape as on a chalkboard
But all nights come to an end
The trio walks into gray morning
Through a gauntlet of garbage cans

Like a raft slipping by
After a night of wine
Dance and laughter
They pass in shadow
Tararaboom ti-ay
Tararaboom ti-ay
Our Lady sings

In the strange logic of gender
It is always the denial that prompts
D to think none are women
Not even Ernestine her mother —
Save a little girl Culafroy
Used to know back home
Solange was her name

Out there on a stone bench
No wider than a hem
They sat together the same
Way — feet tucked, smocks
Pulled tight without a fold
Sometimes they'd go to the Rock
On days when the sky came down

Like blue powder in a water
Glass. Solange would say
"A year from now, a man will jump."
"What man?"
"We don't know. It's someone from far
He must be a hog dealer come to die
Away from the road."

After her convent and pilgrimages
The little seer turned up pretty
Much the same pale voice blond halo
Save she was no longer a part
Of his world; she'd become her own
Self like a work that long ago
Detached from its author

I interrupt myself this morning
To observe a spider weave a web
In the darkest corner of my cell
Having returned to the attic
Divine dons green pajamas
While Our Lady, elbows on knees
Smokes a last cigarette, a mound

Of mossy ruffles at his feet.
"Do you need help with this?"
Divine means the dress which
She starts unlacing in the back
Our Lady somewhat drunk
Lets her strip the prettiest part
Of his name

When he's naked he tumbles
Against Seck and D sees that
Today she'll have to settle
For the outer edge of the bed
That jealousy she felt on Rue Lepic
Worms its way leaving her mouth
Drawn shut like an alligator clutch

Gentle reader forgive me
If I skip the nightly mise-en-scène
Of their bodies pressed tight
At the gate of desire where D's
Cheeks admit entrance to tramps
Bandits and mercenaries without
Once asking "Who goes there?"

But in the final account
Divine rests her head
On the pillow knowing
Full well that the pair has
Played their game it seems
Without her. "C'est la vie,"
Say the old folks

In her deep misery
At being the odd
One out, Divine
Turns to archery and
Our Lady becomes
The burning bush
Of her invectives

I'm not going to keep
Those layabouts, she thinks
While drying her teacups
Hands grasp the axe, a streak
Of dreadful executions
A shock of mutilations
Appear out of nowhere

She drops her kitchen rag
And is back in the crawlspace
Of the human race, but one day
She's had enough; Seck had
Once again forgotten to include her
"Shit, I always think there's only
Two of us."

As so happens, D runs
Into Mimosa, old bat now
"Wowie zowie, I'm crazy
About your Lady
Still so fresh so divine."
"You like her? Want her?"
"Poor girl, she's done with you, eh?"

(Between them, queens
Always used the feminine
To speak of their friends)
"Our Lady's a pain in the ass
Stupid and soft to boot."
"So I can have her for sure?"
"Come to the house for tea."

"You know Roger's off
I'm the Quite-Widow!
You are so sweet, Divine
Let me kiss you, chérie."
Back home she lays out her trap
"Wanna make a hundred francs?"
"Doing what?" Our Lady asks

"Mimosa would like to sleep
With you, an hour or two
Roger's in the army . . ."
"Hell, that's not enough dough."
"Look, she's coming by later on
Make it last, you know the trick
But please don't pinch anything . . ."

Unaware of D's ambush
Our Lady lets the cat out
Of the bag: Gorgui approves
Seeing only the five louis
Reflected in his eyes like small
Miniature fields semy with gold
Still something eludes him

But the assassin is wilier
Than a snake in the grass
Territorial habit you pick up
Like a package or song half
Forgotten
The fact is Our Lady was back
Dealing coke for Marchetti

At times when I'm really down
I can't help but sing certain key
Phrases pimps invent behind
Closed doors. That kind of slang
Turns me inside out like a glove
As I pan with my sluice box
Amidst waste and gravel

For some reason it's Mignon-
Dainty-Feet I recall now
Walking into a department
Store as if pushed by a wave
Mirrors, chandeliers, carpets —
Sole luxury he can touch up close —
Mute the wild pitch of his heart

Another will, another self
Enters his eyes and mouth
Mignon the tough, the mac
Comes to life like a steep rock
Bright with mossy cracks
Where red-tailed birds fly off
In a stretch of sky above

He steals with art
Really, a science
The parabola arc
From showcase to
His pocket demands
Precision. Like falling
Asters or snowflakes

Perfume vials, pipes
And lighters trace
A short curve along
His thighs. Later
On the table he can
Hardly remember
Where they came from

"What have you stolen,
Young man?" a little old
Lady asks quietly.
The address flatters
Otherwise he'd make
A run for it and just like
That, the universe's upon him

The same day he's booked
Thieves, forgers, beggars
And pimps all led on a leash
As in a dream — Black Maria
Headed for Fresnes' house of arrest
I could without changing much
Speak of my life right here and now

At night, as soon as Mignon
Lies down on his bed
The whole prison goes
Topsy-turvy like a crepe
In a pan. His mouth
Is full of stones. Back
Home or in the attic

When he sits, rests
Or takes a cup of tea
He won't ever forget
That he sleeps or rests
On a carcass of a chair
The white tile latrine
The naked bulb that hangs

Dry kelp mattress, narrow
As a bier, chair fastened
To the wall with a chain
All hearken back to a very
Ancient order that shackles
The numb feet of His Majesty's
Galley slaves

Mignon had been in the pen
Three months when he heard
About Our Lady from a kid
In the parlor
Everything I will tell you, A to Z
He'd learnt by bits and scraps
Words whispered behind a hand

Spread like a fan.
Here's the scene:
Our Lady whose dealer
Moniker is Pete the Corsican
And the kid, hear the door bell
"Police!" one of the men says
Turning up his badge

One has to have a pixie soul
To mix everyday life —
Buttons to sew, laces to tie,
Blackheads to squeeze —
With detective novels.
The cops enter at once
Smelling crime

The fact is they're right
Because the kid's studio
Has the same choking air
Roses and arum lilies
On the mantelpiece
As when Our Lady
Strangled the old man

In the middle of the room
A naked body lay flat
The idea of a sham murder
Made the police ill at ease
Yet they quickly see the corpse
Is nothing more than a tailor's
Dummy

All they want is the coke
That one of their snitches
Has tracked down to the kid
"Give me the dope!"
He holds out a tiny packet
"What about him?"
"He's got nothing, chief!"

"What in the hell is that?"
A mannequin. Divine's aura
Hangs like a scarf, absurd
And inexplicable veil.
One night the two kids
Had stolen from a parked car
A cardboard box:

Upon opening it, they found
The dreadful parts of a wax
Doll.
Fake or not cops take both
Back to the station: kicks
In the belly, slaps upside the head
Ribs and other places.

"Confess!" they scream
Finally Our Lady rolls
Under the table
Enraged, a policeman
Dives after him but another
Holds him back by the sleeve
"Let go, Gaubert. It's not like

He killed someone."
"That cute mug? He could
Do it, believe you me!"
Shaking like a leaf
Our Lady crawls out
From underneath
After all, it's just cocaine

"You're not going
To the guillotine,"
The good cop says
Handing him a cig
"The thing that pissed
Him off is your dummy."
Straining against his teeth

The murder confession
Rises in him like smoke
If he opens his mouth now
He's done for, sentenced
To death. I'm only eighteen
I can't die yet, he thinks quickly
God! No! Not a word!

He's safe. The confession
Pulls back like a tide
"I killed the old man."
"What old man?"
Our Lady laughs out loud
"I'm kidding, come on!"
But these people want to know

The detectives shout
Names from the last
Ten years — cold cases
Of violent deaths pass
Before his eyes —
It's a guessing game
"Am I hot? Ragon?"

A drowned child
On the shore
Undone
Incomprehensible
Face
"Yes! That's him."
Everything goes blank.

Overnight, Our Lady
Becomes a sensation
His name a household
Item across all of France
Under the rubric of thefts
Rapes and assaults with
A deadly weapon, the story

Makes the rounds, more
Hypnotic than the fly
Of a dead man
Three inches of print as if
Filled with bloody columns
And torture stakes
Paris won't sleep a wink

Tomorrow Our Lady
Appears in court before
The presiding judge,
Vase de Sainte-Marie.
Red draperies, ermine
Robe and high ceilings
The stage set for a hearing

Since noon the room
Has been filling up
The crowd quivers
Shifts and shuffles
For the circumstance
Where Our Lady dances
On the lip of a chasm

Death here is but a black
Wing, a pirate's flag,
Green crêpe de Chine tie
Only visible evidence
Lies like a handprint
On the judge's desk
Stacked high with files

Between two Republican
Guards, the child enters
I dare to say all eyes
Read the graven words
In his aura: "I am the
Immaculate Conception"
Light gray flannel suit

Blue shirt open at the neck
And that rebel mop in his eyes
Any moment now a trap door
Beneath the judges' feet
Will pull them down
Like fakirs hanging
For an eternity

The guard of honor
In hobnailed boots
Rattling bayonets
Appears on the left
Our Lady mistakes
Them for the firing
Squad

"All rise!"
"Your name is Adrien Baillon?"
"Yes, Your Honor."
"Born December 19th, 1920?"
"Yes, Your Honor."
"Can you give the court
The name you go by?"

Though the murderer
Doesn't answer
The name floats
Winged, secret and fragrant
"On the night of July 7, 1937
You entered the apartment
Of Paul Ragon, aged sixty-seven."

"Do you acknowledge these facts?"
"Yes, sir."
"There was no trace of forced entry
The report states, am I right?
Monsieur Ragon offered you liquor
And with this tie," the judge
Rolls the soft thing like an ectoplasm,

"You strangled the victim.
Do you here recognize
This as the crime weapon?"
"Yes, sir."
"And who gave you the idea
For such a method?"
"He did."

"The murdered man told you
How to eliminate him! Come,
Now, let's be serious!"
A sudden modesty prevents
Our Lady from speaking at once
"Mr. Ragon was wearing a tie
You see. It was too tight . . .

"So I thought if I was to squeeze
It'd be worser," and then barely
Loud enough for the first row
He adds, "cuz I've good arms."
"Good grief! but why, you wretch?"
"I was flat broke, strapped, beat."
The crowd blinks and twists

The twelve men of the jury
Leave through a small side door
"Chin up!" the defense attorney
Says to Our Lady. "You were
Frank and that'll count for us."
The kid's smile made the guards
Believe in God and geometry

The astounding story where
A fake murder leads to a real
One was now easier to accept
Since the manuscript I carried
In my back pocket had been
Stolen by the screw
Outside, snow's falling

One by one, witnesses
Are dropped into the trial,
Raise a hand and swear
"Nothing but the truth."
When Mimosa II steps up
A clerk shouts, "René Hirsch."
For First-Communion

Bewildered, Our Lady
Hears "Antoine Berthollet"
And so our little faggots
From Blanche to Pigalle
Are stripped of their frills
Like a paper flower
In a dancer's hand

The queens now showed
That carcass Our Lady guessed
Under the silk and velvet
Of each armchair
Whether timid or vamp
They no longer bloomed
At the outdoor cafés

Divine, Mimosa, 1st-Communion
Our Lady of the Flowers
How did faggots get these
Noms de guerre?
I didn't choose them at random
A whiff of incense and church
Candle seems to float here

As if I'd picked flowers from
The Virgin Mary's chapel
"Mr. Louis Culafroy," the clerk
Calls out. Leaning on Ernestine —
Only real woman there — Divine
Makes her entrance letting what's
Left of her beauty take a powder

"I do so swear," she too says.
"What do you know about
The defendant?" the judge asks
"Your Honor, I've known him
For a long time. He's sweet
And childlike. He could be
My son."

For the first time in her life
She's taken seriously
In the human parade
The crowd grows restless
As a dog
Death seems to be late.
Finally the medical expert

Approaches the bench
His shifty voice hugs
Certain words: "Unbalanced,"
"Psychopath," "schizophrenia,"
"Freud . . . Jung . . . Adler . . ."
The great psychiatrist glances
At his notes

One gathers this: what's
A criminal? a necktie
Dancing in the moonlight
A vial of poison, gloved
Hands, sailor's blue collar
A series of benign gestures
The dagger that ascends the stairs

Silence falls on the courtroom
Our Lady thinks, "Maybe he
Ain't such a prick, after all."
He's granting his executioner
A premature forgiveness
Then it's the prosecutor's turn
One must protect our retirees

And send to death the children
Who slit their throats
It's all well spoken
With a noble tone
The clock strikes five
"What can you say
In your defense?"

He wants to sound natural
But the answers come in slang
When he knows he ought to speak
French given the circumstance
And then a sentence takes shape
On his lips: "The old man was done for
Couldn't even get a hard-on."

The judge's robe trembles
Three times as if it were
A theater curtain
His defense attorney starts
Babbling about
Thirst and hunger
And the quasi-carnal

Temptation of the neck
He goes on and on
Totally off track
What game is this
Moron playing?
Safe in their seats
The jurors fall for

The corpse of a teen
Whose defense is still
Drooling, now begging
For reform school. We can
Barely hear him
Our Lady says in a sulk,
"I'd rather croak right now."

"Please, ladies and gentlemen,
He's but a child!" and to the kid
"Let me defend you."
Despair had entered him
Like an arrow and all that
Was left now were the white
Rags of his torn heart

He's no longer in
This room, this world
Bareheaded the monocle
Reads the verdict:
"Baillon, alias Our Lady
Of the Flowers, condemned
To capital punishment."

The jury stands up
It's the apotheosis.
Back to the guards
Our Lady seems
To embody the holy
Character of an ancient
Sacrificial victim

Goat, ox or child
Forty days later
On a spring night
The rig was ready
In the prison yard
At dawn Our Lady
Had his head cut

By a real knife.
Nothing happened.
Just because a god
Gives up the ghost
Doesn't mean the veil
Has to be torn
From top to bottom

I've reread my chapters
And notice that not a smile
Was given to Culafroy,
Divine nor the others.
In every child I see
I try to find the one I was
During visits I saw those

Two kids and loved them
For the men they'd become
On their shoulder blades
A ball of muscles already
Covered the tips of their wings
I looked at one's face and eyes
Thinking I could recognize

Myself when boom!
He smiled and no way
Could that be me, too pale
Like a loaf of bread.
Never had I laughed nor
Smiled for that matter and so
Crumbled before the child

Here are the last Divinarias
That you unravel
To read the essential form
Of a saint: her life?
The Valley of Death
With black stormy pines
I travel through in chains

Tic by tic, she detaches
From the human column
Having spent a lifetime
Plunging into the abyss
Now that her body's exiled —
Little bits of skin and bone —
She slips off to heaven

"Lady of High Pansiness"
She calls herself
Or Bernadette Soubirous
At the Charity convent
After her vision
Of the Holy Virgin
Madame, née Secret

Ernestine comes to
Divine's deathbed
And knows from signs
More obvious than a shroud
That only country women
Recognize: "He's leaving,"
She says to herself

Death was so close
That it could touch
D with its index
Finger as if knocking
On a door
But I'm not dead yet
She tells the priest

I heard the angels
Fart on the ceiling
And instantly sees
The old Adeline
Laid out cold on her bed
Culafroy with rigid arms
Lifts the sheets and dares

To kiss the icy lids
The thread starts there
That will lead Culafroy-
Divine to the end
Of course the shuffle,
Hobble and clumsy groping
Had begun much earlier

Here's how our Great
Divine dies
Looking for a gold
Watch that has slid
Between her thighs
Fist closed over
She hands it to Ernestine

Sitting at her bedside
Their two hands make
A shell with the wrist-
Watch in the middle
A vast calm descends
An almost liquid shit
Forms a lake beneath her

And she sinks
Ever so gently
Like a Roman ship
Into the volcanic
Waters of Lake Nemi
And heaves another sigh
Now tinged with blood

Then another: her last
Thus she passed away
One could say drowned
Ernestine who was waiting
Finally grasped that what
Was beating in their joined
Hands was the ticktock of the watch

Not being superstitious she lays
Out the corpse all by herself
Dressing D in a modest blue
Worsted suit of English cut
And there she is the Quite-Dead
White sheets like sails on a vessel
Drifting toward infinity

What possibly could I say
Now that she's no more
My cell so sweet today
Lulled by that kind death
What if I were free?
(Tomorrow the hearing)
Who will be judged?

A stranger whose name
Was once mine?
I can dwell until death
Amongst these widowers
Lamp, washbasin, broom
And the straw pallet
My spouse

I don't feel like sleeping
The wind outside gets
Fiercer by the second
Now rain adds its two cents
I should weep tonight
For my farewell
Rent, the exhausting fraternity

That links me to the dead
I shall live perhaps . . .
And should I be condemned
To the stiffest sentence
I'll invent new lives
For the enchantment of my cell
For Mignon, Divine and Our Lady

Fresnes Prison, 1942

ACKNOWLEDGMENTS

Parts of this text were first published in *Absinthe*, *Eleven Eleven*, *Jacket*, and *Quill Puddle*. My gratitude to the editors.

CHRIS TYSH is the author of several collections of poetry and drama, including, most recently, *Night Scales* (United Artists, 2010) and *Molloy: The Flip Side* (BlazeVox, 2012). A recipient of fellowships from the NEA and the Kresge Foundation, she lives in Detroit and teaches at Wayne State University. *Our Lady of the Flowers, Echoic* is the second volume of her three-part project, *Hotel des Archives*, inspired by the French novels of Samuel Beckett, Jean Genet, and Marguerite Duras.

ROBERT GLÜCK is the author of nine books of poetry and fiction, including two novels, *Margery Kempe* and *Jack the Modernist* and a book of stories, *Denny Smith*. Glück prefaced *Between Life and Death*, a book on the paintings of Frank Moore, and he edited, along with Camille Roy, Mary Berger and Gail Scott, the anthology *Biting The Error: Writers Explore Narrative*. Glück was Co-Director of Small Press Traffic Literary Arts Center, Director of The Poetry Center at San Francisco State, and Associate Editor at Lapis Press. In 2013 Ithuriel's Spear will republish his first book of stories, *Elements*.

ALICE KÖNITZ studied at the Kunstakademie in Düsseldorf and at CalArts. She has presented her work in numerous exhibitions including the 2008 Whitney Biennial (Whitney Museum of American Art, NY); the 2008 California Biennial (Joshua Tree/Orange County Museum of Art); "Half Square Half Crazy," Villa Arson (Nice, France); International Paper (UCLA Hammer Museum, LA); and the Tirana Biennial (Tiranana, Albania). Her solo exhibitions were at Susanne Vielmetter Projects, Los Angeles and Berlin; The University Art Museum, CSU Long Beach; LAXArt, Los Angeles; Hudson Franklin, New York; LACE, Los Angeles, and Luis Campaña, Cologne, Germany. Her work has been reviewed and published in *Artforum, Frieze, Flash Art, Sculpture Magazine, Art and Text, The New York Times, Los Angeles Times*, and other publications.

TRENCHART: LOGISTICS